Vital Signs

poems by

Vincent Casaregola

Finishing Line Press
Georgetown, Kentucky

Vital Signs

For all who struggle with illness or injury,
for all those we have lost,
for all those who remain to mourn them.

Copyright © 2025 by Vincent Casaregola
ISBN 979-8-89990-129-4 First Edition
All rights reserved under International and Pan-American Copyright Conventions. No part of this book may be reproduced in any manner whatsoever without written permission from the publisher, except in the case of brief quotations embodied in critical articles and reviews.

Acknowledgments

I would like to thank the following individuals for their help in reading portions or all of this collection and other pieces of my writing, as well as for all their kindness and help with my work overall. I thank my current colleagues Ron Austin, Dan Finucane, Devin Johnston, and Ted Mathys. I thank my retired colleagues Paul Acker, Jan McIntire-Strasberg, and Sara van den Berg, along with colleagues at other universities, including Robert Blaskiewicz, Matt Diomede, Sarah Fielding, Paul Stabile, and Lauren Schwarz. I am also grateful to my fellow poets Dwight Bitikofer, Ryan Bry, and Matt Freeman for their inspiration and encouragement, along with that of journal editors Aaron Lelito (poetry editor of *The Closed Eye Open*) and Deirdre Neilen (Editor, *The Healing Muse*). Never far from my mind is the debt I owe to my late colleagues, Ray Benoit, Lou Fournier, and James Scott, who were always available for help and encouragement. My long-time friend, fellow teacher, and fellow writer, Pat Mannix, has always been an inspiration and a guide to whom I could turn with any questions or concerns. And of course, my wife Victoria and daughters Maya and Marina give me the unconditional love and support that makes my writing possible.

Publisher: Leah Huete de Maines
Editor: Christen Kincaid
Author Photo: Vincent Casaregola
Cover Design: Elizabeth Maines McCleavy

Order online: www.finishinglinepress.com
also available on amazon.com

Author inquiries and mail orders:
Finishing Line Press
PO Box 1626
Georgetown, Kentucky 40324
USA

Contents

Prefatory Note ix

I—The Site of the Trauma

As If Secrets Would Spill 1
In the Sunlight 2
The Ceremony of Innocence 3
What the Bullet Knows 4
In the Heat of the Moon 5
Emergency Procedure Guide 7
Chicago View 9
Coventry Carol 10
The Mummy's Curse 12
Threnody for the Missing 14
Imminent Disaster 15
Specific Gravity 16

II—Critical Cares

"Never Send . . ." 19
"Mystic Chords of Memory" 21
Carbon Content 23
Life of the Ball Turret Gunner 24
The Face in the Memory Mirror 26
This Poem Is Just *about* You 27
Death, I Fear, Is Always in the Middle 29
Respiratory Monitor 30
Prostrate 31
Holiday Rush 33
Call It 34
When He Died in His Sleep 36
Everyman Revisited 38
Odonata 42
There Is Nothing to Say 44
Transmigration of Souls 46

III—The Case History Monologues

1. Clinical in Creve Coeur 51
2. Work-in-Progress 53
3. Understanding Depression 55

4. The Matter of Perception 56
5. Graveyard Shift 58
6. Street 59
7. Sanctuary 60
8. Quiet 62
9. Excited 64
10. Riddle of the Open Heart 67

IV—In the Shadow of Corona

Going Viral 71
The Silence 72
A Social Distance 73
Six 74
Fragments in COVID Time 75
What Darkness May Come 78
Birdman 79
Descent into the Underworld 80
What Will You Remember 81
When It Will Come 82
Where Is the Shadow? 84
Lethe 85

Prefatory Note

Vital Signs is a collection of poetry that explores the experience of trauma, injury, illness, and related areas. It is divided into four parts. Part I, "The Site of the Trauma," examines the physical and psychological traumas of urban stress, accidents, poverty, crime, and the associated illnesses and injuries. Part II, "Critical Cares" focuses on the experiences of illness and health care from the perspectives of patients, family caregivers, health care workers, and others. Part III, "The Case History Monologues" gives voice to those who suffer illness, especially mental illness, and the painful consequences that may come from such suffering. Finally, Part IV, "In the Shadow of Corona," confronts the many traumatic aspects of the COVID-19 pandemic, especially the new immediacy of dealing with death and loss both near and far. Together, these clusters of poems present a range of perspectives on the experience of illness/injury, health care, loss, and grieving, all of which are "vital signs" of the current condition of our culture.

I. The Site of the Trauma*

---

*"Returning to the scene of the trauma is often recommended as part of trauma-focused cognitive-behavioural therapies for post-traumatic stress disorder (PTSD)." [Hannah Murray, Christopher Merritt, and Nick Grey—"Returning to the scene of the trauma in PTSD treatment—why, how and when?" in *the Cognitive Behavioral Therapist*, Volume 8, e28.]

As If Secrets Would Spill

Of course I look, just as you,
though neither will admit to it—
as if secrets would spill,
or some message might appear
from the icon of a body
stretched silent on the pavement.

We are drawn in, first, by lights
that ring the scene like a tragic
Christmas wreath in red, blue,
yellow and green, making me blink
so strong their contrast to the night—
a cluster of EMTs still hovers like
frightened birds near a broken nest.

I see only the prone form,
spread-eagled, art for passers-by,
an elegy in the making—
if I could draw closer, I would,
to see a final look in the eyes
that might be seeing something
"new and strange," or to hear,
a last broken gasp of revelation—

but nothing, now or later, but harsh light
and cluttered sounds, and customers
still passing through the Shell station—
nothing, but the stories we may craft
from shadows, to be echoed by
the morning news—"he died crossing
against the light and wearing dark clothing."

Officers cordon the area with
long yellow ribbons of warning,
while others measure distances, to solve
the calculus of death on a dark street—
they, too, can gather only facts,
no solace, no insight, no comfort for those
who drive past in search of more.

In the Sunlight

Black letters, "Do Not Cross,"
on shiny yellow tape, rising and
falling on the afternoon breeze,
rustling, surrounding the site

Bright yellow, with black numbers,
the bent plastic markers, just like
what restaurants use to tag the order,
scattered randomly on black asphalt

Brass casings, cast like seed
on hard ground, some still smooth,
some dented, but each one shining
in the hot, late-summer sun.

The Ceremony of Innocence

". . . everywhere the ceremony of innocence is drowned . . ."
    —W. B. Yeats

In the rain, pale chalk handprints,
yellow and blue pastel, melt
and fade to uneven green,
bleeding down the driveway apron,
running fast to the waiting street.

On sidewalk squares, the hopscotch
grid blurs and flows away, leaving
just faint memories of digits
and once-straight lines, its simple
meaning now forever gnostic.

On the street, orange cones circle, linked
by yellow tape with black letters, as wind
curves the tape to shallow gutters that
catch rain running to rivulets, cascading
to the cracked and broken pavement.

In the rain, all flows downward,
spilled blood and oil blend
in water that, once clear, now clouds,
speeding through drains and dark sewers
to the obscure river miles beyond.

What the Bullet Knows

Still new, the bullet knows,
innocently enough,
its own weight and heft,
solid and compact, smooth
and curved like a statue,
touched with power—
a totem or fetish.

The bullet learns,
soon enough, to be patient,
to wait in its tight jacket,
snug in its casing, waiting
with its brothers, all servants
to some deep and sudden will.

The bullet knows its own fire,
its sudden freedom of speed,
out in the open at last,
stinging the air till
that air itself is smoke,
wild with red and yellow light.

But the bullet is shocked
by its own trajectory and impact,
appalled at diving deep
into liquid red shadows,
into caves of bone that crack
like stalactites and shatter
downward into night.

The bullet cries out
in its own shattering demise
because it did not yet know
how to kill and die
in the same instant,
in a dozen jagged parts
fanning out, slowing down,
each tearing into its own red grave.

In the Heat of the Moon

[Ferguson, Missouri—August 2014]

Late summer days, relentless sun
heating the morning city, turning
afternoon to a concrete sauna
during the searing days of August,
when, even at night, the asphalt steams.

Nowhere to hide, these days,
from the scent or sight of ourselves,
no one else to blame in the stark light,
for what we have always known of rage
rippling across red sunburnt skin.

It's said that war's first casualty is truth,
and this even in undeclared wars
of color, class, or cold contempt
that scar the city streets with blood
and the angry glint of broken glass.

A body, lying in the hot street, spills
itself across our memory, burns
its image in even the denying heart—
its own truth too raw to name at first,
its silent cry lost amid the sirens.

We can never know the final thoughts
of the young man falling through the heat,
to singe his dark skin on hot pavement,
feeling bullets carve his body, flashing
light and dark across his shattered brain.

We can never know what angry, hidden will,
what frenzied pulse, kept the finger
pulling shot after shot from the leaping gun,
as if the officer were watching his own hand
become an alien being intent to kill.

We did not hear the gasping breath or
feel the throbbing muscles as the gun
relaxed and air grew screaming silent,
could not see with unblinking eyes
what hands had wrought in the angry sun.

Gasping, too, the man inert on the ground,
spreading his dark red shadow behind
head and shoulders, the last breaths
rattling then fading, the final twitch
as nerves refused to go quietly away.

Bodies turn to numbers in the strange
calculus of distance and time,
but the numbers keep climbing faster,
like tallies in some cruel machine,
that computes the endless cost of hate.

It has all happened in the time
of the "super moon" that in its perigee
came so close it must have pulled
our reason far into the cloudless dark,
leaving just the sudden urge to strike.

"Emergency Procedure Guide"

[Distributed by the Public Safety Authority for our building.] *

It begins with "Fire" and ends
with "Sounds like a Gunshot,"
encompassing, on one laminated sheet,
the full array of terror and loss,
along with all the numbers to call
for help and deliverance.

Tempests, heart attacks, and even
the fearful quaking earth itself,
along with the possible failure
of any and all the powers and
machines to which we hold ourselves
mere subjects and attendants—all,
all are foreseen and listed
in this catalog of disaster.

Concluding with the violence
we can hold at once in both
our shaking hands and
trembling souls, it recites
the best response to the sound—
the "loud report" that might not,
just might not, be a car backfiring
or a metal door slammed shut.

Shut but do not slam your doors,
turn off the lights and in the dark
hide where you cannot be seen—
disappear, like the frightened animal
fleeing the hunter, like the child
fearing the monsters of dreams.

And, despite the obvious impulse
to seek the comfort and warmth
of fellow beings so threatened,
do not, we repeat, do not
huddle together, making each shot
a multiple killer—suffer, rather,
in silent isolation, texting perhaps,
the precise location of the incident.

If you remain on a ground floor,
the windows, if they open, can offer
escape and salvation, but if not,
do not attempt to exit through the halls,
where a troubled soul grasps,
like a last straw, the easiest means
of available expression, persuaded
that only this loud but wordless
utterance can serve his ragged will.

Some say he answers hidden voices,
others will call him plainly evil,
and others still—envying the power
he clutches so firmly and deftly,
even in his final desperation—they
would have you grasp it likewise,
filling the halls with ricocheting
sound and spinning fury, until
the single song of death becomes
a great Greek chorus, chanting
for demise, bringing on the gods,
until the whole play tumbles down
to full catastrophe, and one,
just one, tragic mask, echoing
the same emphatic cry, remains.

---

*Since this Guide was first issued, the Authority has revised its stance, encouraging building occupants not to hide but to flee or, if possible, to fight back with what means are available.

Chicago View

You can stare out this fourth-floor
back window and see the El tracks,
dry snow dusting between the ties
and rails, leading to the windswept
empty platform, early Saturday.

Backs of buildings repeat the same
silence, row by row, block by block,
back windows unmoved, staring back,
balconies and stairs, paint-chipped,
sagging with a history not written.

The bricks have nothing to say,
remaining in place, like soldiers
in formation, they serve to stand
and wait, and to keep watch—on
back lots, on old cars, on rooftops.

What life goes on, goes on in hiding,
from bitter wind and ill-intentioned
fate, from what desire or danger
or mere despair is blown up
the alleyways and into crevices

in old concrete walls by the El.
What life goes on lives furtively,
fitfully, bracing against the sting
of cold air on that colder wind.
What life goes on reveals itself

subtly—the steam from that vent
pipe on the roof, the motion
of slow-walking people, bundled,
hiding any spark within, hoping
to preserve light in winter grimness.

The El collects itself along the platform,
then departs, its cars, once silver,
now tarnished to grey, but still
sparking blue-white from the third rail,
a flash of light and a threat of death.

Coventry Carol

A cold, lake-effect wind blows up
the hill of a street called Coventry,
and ruffles the torn trouser cuffs
of Mr. J as he descends into night.

Ill-shod feet pad sidewalk squares
with worn soles of a worn soul,
feet that had once tapped the rhythm
to a mellow sound from his shiny horn.

He'd grown up on old LPs, recordings
of Trane and Bird and Sonny Rollins,
fingering his own tunes by eleven,
playing in clubs at seventeen.

Those days were hope days of vision,
bright with high notes, dark with low tones,
in the last of the real clubs, gone one
by one, till only studio work remained.

For money, he took the jobs he could—
for wife and kids, for food and clothes,
and almost a decent place to live—
but he could take it for only so long,

playing backing for sessions, sideman
for someone else's shows, till pride
washed away with glasses and bottles,
till work thinned down, trickled out.

Ago long time was his plaintive,
mournful horn, now long pawned,
or sold, he can't remember which—
wife gone with the diabetes to the grave,

and of four kids, two survived the
the horror-carved narrow streets
of the slugged out, drugged out hood,
and one went east, one went west,

leaving him in his cuckoo's nest—
so be it, said the old corner preacher,
yesterday, in broad daylight, and now
here it is the night of awaiting dawn.

Nearing the bottom of the hill,
he'll turn right, heading for the bridge
that'll keep off some of the snow,
with a side wall that blocks the wind.

His duffle holds a blanket patched
with bits of duct tape, along with
an old square of blue plastic tarp—
he'll soon bed down with these.

From two blocks away, carols
from speakers in a parking lot,
sharp sounds rattling, annoy his ears,
but he takes any music port in a storm.

Who knows tomorrow—a cold dawn
with back stiff and stomach blank,
or maybe just the quiet of the ending,
after that last note, before the applause?

The Mummy's Curse

The one who found him
worked for the state—an engineer
with DOT, inspecting bridges.
White helmet and yellow vest,
he'd take his flashlight
in dark and hidden places
to check concrete and steel members
for cracking, spalling, and stains of rust.

Beneath the span, he'd often found
so much discarded, mostly trash,
but this was his first finding
a man, or what was left—he
lifted the ragged edge of old
blue tarp, and curled beneath
was the old man, or seeming old.

How can you tell at that point,
pale with age, illness, or both,
blue at the edges from cold,
a face taut with the restraint
of the slow frozen night? The image,
as if from a surreal painting,
would remain buried in the mind.

Curved into a final, fetal shape,
wearing an old, stained parka,
the lining puffing out from tears,
and a dark blue watch cap, ragged,
pulled down around the ears, he
seemed some lost sailor, recently
washed up from a deep grave.

The EMTs found it hard
to move the body, tightly held
in its shrunken form, a closed fist—
the skin had shrunk around bone,
"like a mummy looks," said one,
with a brief uncaring laugh,
inured now to death in any form.

The engineer shivered, backed off,
having found a crack he could not fix,
a problem closed but never solved—
he quickly returned to work,
but the blue-white face remained,
frozen and silent, whenever he closed
his eyes or tried to seek his rest.

From then, his dreams expanded,
and every night he saw a vast globe,
a child's rubber ball grown huge,
crisscrossed with infinite tiny cracks,
and each one held a woman or a man,
prisoners pushing against the weight
and pressure, losing breath, unable
to escape, or even to relax and die.

Threnody for the Missing

You are shopping late at night
in the near-empty grocery,
when most have already gone to bed,
and only then do you really hear the voice,
only then see the missing face.

Oh, yes, the posters and images
remain perpetually—on milk cartons,
on the bench out front by the bus stop,
and even on the community bulletin board,
among the flyers for services
like dog grooming and yoga class.

In the chilled white space of the dairy aisle,
you pick up the carton, cold to the touch,
moist with condensation, and turn it
to see the shy face a decade old,
with the haunting cliché "last seen on . . ."

At the checkout counter, more images
with sad and desperate phrasing—
"He suffers from a health condition
and must have his medication," and that
was 15 years ago, when he was three.
Another flyer claims "This image shows
what she might look like today," ten years
after never returning home from school.

You walk slowly out the door, a bag
heavy in each hand, imagining the father
who wakes daily at 3 a.m. and stares,
for a full hour, out the bedroom window,
or the mother who combs the web
for news of every kidnapped girl
recovered fifteen years later
from some blank suburban house.

Imminent Disaster

Grabbing for keys in the bowl
by the front door, thinking only
of getting to work on time,
he did not know that semi, running
late, would miss the light,
cutting his car in two.

Waiting to board, he did not
anticipate that errant part,
a turbine blade, would pick
this day to fatigue and fail,
bursting from the engine and
tearing fire through the wing.

The day seemed calm, and boating
more calming still, no danger
in placid waters, unhurried
by the wind, but then again,
the shoals and rocks keep
silent till they crack a hull.

Even in a common back yard,
where debris from last night's
storm lay scattered, he did not sense
that the web of branches held
a wire still waiting for his touch.

And stopping late at 7-Eleven,
just to grab a cold Dr. Pepper
on one more hot July night,
he did not suspect the bullet,
ill-aimed, would take him out.

Specific Gravity

It must be the bones, endless
and fragmented, some bleached
in relentless angry sun,
some mineral-darkened with age,
and most ground to fine powder
that may irritate the eye and skin.

Over time, the bones increase
the planet's weight, its mass,
though no expert or agency
confirms this transformation;
still, our globe takes on the burden
gradually distorting its shape,
infecting its depths.

We sense but cannot name
such increasing gravity
pulling us earthwards, calling us down,
but old Zia Annunziata,
whom the children called "Strega A,"
would stare sadly at the floor,
her sun-browned, wrinkled hands folded
in the lap of her faded black dress,
and in her crackling, aged voice,
say softly, but with certainty,
"the bones, tonight, lie heavy in the earth."

II—Critical Cares*

*"Critical care medicine encompasses the diagnosis and treatment of a wide variety of clinical problems representing the extreme of human disease."
[The American College of Physicians Website.]

"Never send . . ."

Having left work early this spring
afternoon, I feel no rush
to be anywhere but here and now,
even waiting at this reluctant light,

where I can watch the warm day pass
casually, like steady traffic,
unhurried by demands of other times
or places—when from the left,

cresting the brow of the hill,
an ambulance appears, flashing
not only its lights but its red self,
proceeding fast but cautiously

through the intersection,
its red seeming so intense and loud
against the crisp blue of sky and
dull browns and ochres of walls.

It passes beneath the electronic
billboard, where each ad lasts but
thirty seconds, and now we see
"The Alliance of Furriers" who

represent their arts with the image
of a woman in lingerie, cloaking
herself in an ankle-length white coat
of mink or fox. No matter,

the ambulance and cargo proceed,
giving me the impulse to pray
to a God increasingly obscure
(God never prays, you know,

perhaps does not know how),
but my prayer is an attempt to see
in mind's eye the interior in pastel
green or blue, where EMTs rush

to attach tubes and wires to the proper
spots of flesh. Why, I wonder, and who
takes this frantic ride, perhaps the last,
as the red shape disappears beneath

the highway bridge to the right—
I imagine the child gasping through
the asthma attack without relief,
the old woman in diabetic coma,

the roofer whose one careless step
brought him to ground with crushed hip,
the wife and mother in prime of life
left frozen, staring, speechless,

the aneurysm a blood-red rose
blooming deep within her brain—
I see, as well, my own time come,
when lying dazed and alarmed,

I watch blue-gloved attendants
insert IVs in hand or arm, and I turn
from them to the bland ceiling, uncertain,
trying to sort the images to some point,

and looking past one man's hairy forearm,
I wonder briefly at marvels held
within each tiny wall compartment,
even as my vision blurs and fades.

"Mystic Chords of Memory"

As a child, she was taken
to re-enactments every spring
and summer, whether or not
she really wished to see the old war
fought again, now by men middle-aged,
whom she'd seen more often in feed caps.

Hot July sun made her pale skin
prickly with the coming burn
in those days before all wore sunscreen,
and his hand, rough from working
on tractors or trucks, calloused
from grasping this or that wrench too long,
would pull her along, through high grass
and thistles that stung her bare legs.

The gunpowder made a blue smoke,
made her throat hurt and eyes tear up,
but at least she could see the horses,
graceful, with brown flanks glistening
in the sun, prancing and snorting
under the reins, impatient to play—
he'd wink at her when he caught her
smiling at the horses, knowing he'd won.

It all comes back last week, opening an old box
secreted in the corner of her closet—
inside, a variety of ancient relics, among them
a small scented square, wrapped in old paper,
the soap he'd bought her in the sutler's tent
from the smiling old women in period dress.
Opening the paper, she smells history
along with the faint scent of lilac.

It propelled her, once more, across the continent,
to wait again in the living room, part museum,
part tomb, where the collected objects
arrange themselves for any story
she might want to tell. It takes him
twenty minutes to get back from the bathroom,
the walker clicking before him,
announcing his coming, his finality.

Awkward in the evening light, with sofa cushions
musty and faded, she leans back,
trying to talk about the stroke, the therapy,
and even, God forbid, the possibility
he might move East with her.
He nods, winks, knows something,
or thinks he does, knows at least
that the wink meant something once.
His head droops, then, and he dozes,
while she waits, watching the sunset
reflected in the polished stock
of the musket hanging from the mantel,
in case anyone needs to fight that war again.

The Carbon Content

For my father and his generation

It was a steel town then—
steel, cars, and chemicals—
where men who'd survived
depression, then war,
forged pigs and ingots
and fashioned them into cars.
The morning air smelled
of sulphurous hell and prosperity.
Some ad-man had called it
"the best location in the nation,"
but the steel men paid him no mind.
They had work, neighborhoods,
children, wives, and
tools in the basement.
They drank Black Label at the VFW,
smoked and argued at the union halls,
and panelled a rathskeller as a hideaway.

On odd nights,
they might wake at 3:00 a.m.,
to the creak of the house settling,
to the groan of the furnace in winter.
Then sleep would not return,
and they'd recall the ones lost
across continents, across oceans—
names, faces fading from memory
as from old newspapers.
Even now, death was no stranger—
on the job a missed step, lost balance,
could send a man into the inferno.
They joked grimly of the carbon content
added to the molten mix—
the union paid for the funerals.
Afterwards, in private, each man
looked at his own hands,
the carbon under every finger nail,
knew himself to be chemicals, elemental.

The Life of the Ball Turret Gunner

After Randall Jarrell

The sound of his own anxious breath,
labored in the tightening mask,
seems his whole fearful world
in this moment when, encircled by the dark,
he cannot remember where he is.

Why darkness? Then his eyes open,
revealing not the glass and metal cage
that once had trapped and sheltered him
but this somber grey-white room,
filled with monitors and tubes.

It is now, not then, and death
becomes the old acquaintance,
clicking through the room with a cane,
smiling, then nodding, and passing by—
how did death get so old and still not die?

Then, lifetimes before, he'd folded
himself, fetal and fretting,
butt facing the earth, as he'd waited,
with eyes growing cold from seeing
the endlessness of pale blue air.

That air had soon rattled and roared
when the black bursts of smoky flak
had flowered across the indifferent blue—
he'd shake in his cocoon, with chilly waves
of sweat across his gooseflesh skin.

He'd watched the other planes,
hit and falling through the air,
broken like injured birds or ill-used toys—
a wing spiraling downward, and the rest
sliding endlessly to fiery hell.

Sometimes he'd see the chutes, for
just a moment his chest relaxing,
till he'd see, as well, a body, spread-eagled,
spiraling down like a penny top—a silent
scream of motion through the empty space.

So it had been, long ago, when fragile
and young he'd hung in the air
like a circus trick gone sour with fear
and watched fighters streak across his sights
in their sudden twinkling flash.

Now nothing streaks, and if it did,
he could not see it well enough to know—
though once he'd flown the long transit
from Britain to the angry Reich,
and made it back each time—

each time, come home, landing with
the whole plane shaking, bouncing,
and after every trip they'd paint a bomb
along the nose, so anyone could count
the time and distance back to life.

Well, this was life, what's left,
as he makes a different transit now,
almost weekly, from skilled nursing to
intensive care, and back again
when nurses see his signs improve.

Back then, longing for the final mission,
he feared to think of anything
that he could call a home—lived instead
for moments of pure sensation,

a taste on the tongue or light filtering
across the curve of an exhausted eye—
lived only for each slight impression,
as if his mind had been a gallery
hung with frozen moments of his life.

Now he wants to cease these missions, too,
and closing those same eyes, thinks that time
should finally grant release, send him home—
but no, not yet, and so he blinks awake
and steels himself to hear his anxious breath,
labored in the tightening mask.

The Face in the Memory Mirror

After Vermeer's "Girl with the Pearl Earring"

The mirror is a quiet space,
reflecting the orbed earring
so smooth and delicate
that itself mirrors the small circles
of light hovering in the eyes—
eyes holding their light,
betraying no secret yet.

The scarf wraps her head
with such grace and elegance
that we imagine hair ready to cascade,
curling down upon the shoulders,
giving itself to some
fragrant and exotic wind.

The casual observer knows little
of such guise, or of the smooth orb
the skull becomes, bereft of hair
for weeks past—the treatment's price.

She remembers paintings studied
as a girl in school and this one girl's face,
as smooth as once her own had been,
with Vermeer's magic touch of light,
and color gently shading form.

She recalls and wishes for a skin
so light and smooth to touch
a painter's heart and mind—not
the parchment flesh she wears today
when morning by morning
the mirrors betray her.

That face, those eyes emerge again
from memory, and always
the tiny orbs of light captured
in the pearled jewel and patient gaze,
so powerful that few will see
that framing the whole
is a shapeless wall of black.

This Poem Is Just *about* You

This poem is just *about* you, not you,
not some substitute to hold you
out of time's reach and cost—

this poem cannot touch you, cannot
feel the softness of your skin beneath
a fleeting brush of fingers,

cannot reclaim the sight of you
reclining on a chaise or standing
in the window's morning light,

cannot be the light reflected
in your glance across the table
or be the gentle tilt of your head

when listening, or speak your thoughts
with your voice, tender or alarmed,
angry or soft, as moods propel—

no, this is a thing of words, poor
currency that barely pays the price
of simple goods on ordinary days,

passing words, mortal and fleeting,
with no eternity in store, no marble
meaning etched in history—

and when your rebel cells collude
again, rise in secret, then strike,
bringing insurrection to the lung

or brain, these words bring no relief
from any throbbing pain, no salve
for the sting of doubt and fear

as you, sleepless, outstare
the darkened midnight ceiling, nor
can they ease the ache that grows

stronger with each morning, or feel
the tangled tightness in your grip
as you reach for help to cross a room

these words bring me no comfort,
not even cold comfort, but lie
dry as old paper in the musty attic,

less comfort, even, than a cold,
post-mortem final kiss that seals
the moment in the dim, grey room—

these words themselves have little or no
life, no breath for me to hear as from you
when you'd lain asleep beside me,

and they will fade, as ink on paper fades
in heat and angry sun, or as screens will
fade when the grid itself will die—

carve them on our stones, if you will,
the stones themselves erode to dust,
and even while they last, the sharp carving

smooths with age, making words clefts
for blown sand, for spores of lower plants,
for fibers of what, once, had flowered.

Death, I Fear, Is Always in the Middle

Death, I fear, is always in the middle,
the mediator with a stopwatch,
ultimate arbiter of all disputes,
referee of every temporal game,
judge of each contest or debate—

it is the fog-shrouded river valley
between these distant ridges, where
only strange tree-tops emerge from mist
and stranger sounds, cries or prayers,

and between us in the moment of passion,
the space our bodies transit for love,
arms open to embrace, lips to kiss,
yet eyes closed, afraid to witness death—

a cosmic mystery, a black hole,
the closer we embrace, the dearer love,
the deeper the vastness we encounter,
great abyss, deep gravity of loss—

I caress you, so touch mortality,
sense the passing, moment by moment,
of sense, to soul, to silence or rest,
so hold tight, love, and know the cost
that Death is always in the middle.

Respiratory Monitor

They have softened the room's light
to near dusk, matching the mood—
and the machines speak their lines
in a concert of soft pulses, while
the monitor tracks the vitals
across its impassive face.

Breath, that can barely be heard
by the tired natural ear
of the drowsing, aged spouse
who sits in the bedside chair,
is loud enough for hidden sensors
in the omniscient machine.

Look, the line traces hills
and valleys as a soul continues
its last steps, its arduous course.
The lighted spot ascends and drops
methodically, like an ancient monk
in a far kingdom, journeying
up and down steep mountains,
for a wisdom even he, in his
antiquity, has yet to comprehend.

Prostrate

Words eluded me, changing shape
when, as a small child, I struggled to read—
they'd shift their letters before my eyes,
morph to similar but different forms,

like the words "what" and "want,"
where h and n would shift positions,
extending or retracting that long arm,
so desire and the desired were almost one.

Such errors drew angry faces from
aging nuns who sought perfection
in the young, then bent to give
correction through the rod or rosary.

They also read aloud to us of saints' lives,
filled with words we'd mispronounce,
so we remained muted and silent to hear,
uncomprehending, such bright tales.

"And so he lay prostrate in faith and fear
before the almighty Lord of hosts . . ."—
a line I remembered for that strange word,
but familiar, too, from another place.

"Prostrate," was that not the word
for what ailed my grandfather who,
awaiting his surgery, must lie "prostrate"
before the Lord or at least the surgeons?

We'd visit the hospital, parents entering,
my elder brother watching me, down in
the parking lot—children forbidden, since
we were carriers of sinful germs—

once, he waved from the window, now
erect and no longer prostrate after all.
But today, sixty years since, my turn
arrives, as I lie prostrate for the exam . . .

The young doctor, calm and confident,
reassures with glance and touch, "Don't
worry, we've got this—success rate
is over ninety percent for this stage."

Not much to be lost but these small
sacks of fertilizer, long past any use,
something left behind in the old barn
of this body, souring in the musty cold.

"Go home now, rest, it will be ok . . ."
At home, I speak little, find no rest,
staring through the ceiling to imagined stars,
lying "prostrate" in faith and fear.

Holiday Rush

It all rolled together,
like the space in the windshield—
the turning landscape, end over end,
as they spun and shuddered,
then stopped, like a broken toy,
atilt in the ditch.

All is rearranged, all forgotten, too—
the worry of meals to cook, or halls
to decorate, or shopping left undone—
all lost in the new ice of fear
and the angry rant of pain,
lost, too, in the growing fog of shock.

Soon, all is simplified,
and not even dreams persist
in the soft grey light
and the subtle hum and click
of attendant machines
in a room of wires and tubes.

Down the hall, a hidden speaker
sings, once more, the usual carols,
while the charge nurse sits at her screen,
smiling like Solomon, and plans
the staffing spreadsheet for
for Christmas Eve and morning.

Call It

No one will know, now, or care
that, in your rush this morning,
you grabbed one dark blue sock
and one black in the rumpled sock drawer.

Now stockinged feet rest, splayed, pointing
to opposing walls of the E.R. room,
empty now from its bustling rhythms
just moments before—finally at rest.

The sheet covers you, but not your feet,
and the room surveys you, indifferently,
as one more piece of human furniture
awaiting delivery to another site.

The wall clock continues its measured pace,
its face impassive—it did not stop
when the attending ceased compressions
and told the charge nurse to "call it."

On the floor beside your resting place
lie one crumpled blue glove and three
torn plastic wrappers that had held objects
once thought essential for your survival.

Within you, anatomy is closing down—
lungs, stilled, no longer trouble the air
with gasps, heart machinery motionless,
blood settling in its silent chambers.

Throughout miles of inner vessels,
red cells float aimlessly, and now that
the vital flow has ceased, they sift slowly
downward, sadly, in gravity's firm grasp.

In the brain, electric currents flicker
for a moment, with power now lost,
and section by section neurons fade,
darken themselves, erasing memory.

Tubes dangle from this or that device,
one or two still attached to nose and arm—
linens, blue and white, retain their wrinkles
as you left them, scented of your sweat.

From one wall, the sprinkler system head
remains unperturbed, its chrome housing,
cylindrical, offering back a convex
reflection of your now-pale repose.

Lying here, you remain in this moment's
near silence—only the subtle sounds of air
through the building's pipes—in just a minute,
in will come attendants to wheel you out.

Your mild scent fades from the air, and
your image dissolves, softly, from the memory
of beige walls and grey machines—with you
gone, this room awaits another life or death.

When He Died in His Sleep

When he died in his sleep,
they said it was peaceful, a blessing,
but they did not know his dreams.

When he died in his sleep,
he was dreaming for sure,
dreaming of a cat drinking water,
wondering, while he dreamed,
why he should dream of a cat
drinking water—in the dream itself
he was, as usual, awestruck
at how any animal could drink
so swiftly and magically.

The act had always mystified him,
as did most acts of cats,
but especially that gesture of the tongue,
so quick and silent, like
a language of water and thirst
he could never comprehend.

Never comprehend, not even
when his wife had tried, again
and again, to explain it—
something about the motion
and the muscle and the nerves—
he would ask, and she, patiently,
would explain once more.

As he watched the dream cat,
his wife's image came once more
into the corner of his dream,
a translucent shadow
that made him pause.

She had been catlike, too,
feline and mystifying,
shadow against a shadowy dark,
keeping her mysteries behind
a furtive glance and sly smile.

As he stared at the cat,
the creature looked up, jumping
into his lap and curling there,
staring back, wide-eyed.

But suddenly, the roles reversed,
and he saw now, through cat's eyes,
the old man nodding into sleep,
and catlike he waited, wondering
at the strange beast with stranger scents.

Now the mystery was his, at last,
and though he sensed it,
he could no longer name it,
no more than he could name the wind.

He sensed, as well, the leaving,
the closing down of the once great beast,
he waited still, but losing patience,
catlike, leapt away at last.

When he died in his sleep,
they wept and prayed and sang,
and saw him, in a mind's eye,
rising and walking to the light.

They did not see him, catlike,
leap away once more, and run
to mysteries unseen, unspoken,
shadow on the shadowed night.

Everyman Revisited

I

When I imagine her now,
death coming for me that is,
I see the day work differently—
we have an appointment
for late morning, allowing me
to grow accustomed to the change.

I arrive refreshed
at her offices, which are tasteful
and well-appointed, in shades
of light wood and with extensive
windows for natural light.

She dresses with quiet elegance,
conservative but not somber,
her blue business suit not too dark,
and accented with a delicate scarf
in red, gold and iridescent green.

She rises and shakes my hand,
putting me, immediately, at ease
(it's clear that she is
"client-centered" in her work).
We review the plans, with more
than sufficient time for questions.

She takes me to lunch next door,
a Mediterranean place where,
if you forgive the pun,
the pasta primavera is to die for—
afterwards, with the room to ourselves,
we talk quietly, her face betraying
just the hint of a smile
as I recount my more cherished
anecdotes and memories.

Back in the office, we finalize,
and I sign each copy,
as a prophet witnesses
and an angel serves as notary.

Then the four of us ride together
to the airport, her Lexus not black,
as I would have thought,
but a modest grey, with leather seats.
I open the travel documents,
and, to my delight, I see
that I am flying home,
finally, in first class.

II

Just a pipe dream, I know—
it's really nothing like that, but
rather squalid in fact, as we
wait, two dozen of us,
in that musty room, painted
an institutional green
I haven't seen since grammar school,
and forced to sit in plastic chairs,
many cracked, dingy with age,
and vaguely sticky to the touch.

We refuse to look one another
in the eye, staring instead
at the floor of old linoleum,
knowing each other only
by our frayed cuffs, our
swollen ankles, our scuffed shoes.

A frosted glass window opens,
revealing the bars of a "teller's cage,"
and from the other room, a voice
calls each of us to fill the forms—
Death the clerk is not hostile,
just perfunctory, tired,
and impatient with our
ignorance of procedure.

Finally, my turn comes, and
I rise to greet him—but he doesn't
even look up—a middle-aged
bureaucrat in a bad tie, who merely

slides the documents through
that little trough beneath the bars,
for me to sign and certify.

Then he drops all the forms
into an old office mailer,
with only one address space left,
and he carefully wraps the red string
around those annoying little holders.

He never meets my eyes
but points to the exit,
a dented metal door out back.
Once outside, I line up
with the others as we wait
again, this time to board
an aging bus in faded grey
with "Department of Corrections"
still painted on the side.

III

Then again, perhaps death comes,
not with a human face at all,
but as some generic email
that doesn't even use my name:

"If you have received this message,
then you have recently ceased
to breathe, ceased to be resident
in the created world.

"Do not reply directly
to this message but click
on the link below to confirm
your receipt of this final notice
and your willingness to comply.

"If you feel that you have
received this message in error,
click on the second link to go
to the appeals website."

But when I do, I find
the deadline for appeals
expired one full week ago.

So I stare at the screen, hoping
and then saying aloud,

"It's only spam, it must be spam"—
a joke from some hacker
half way around the globe.

But then the screen freezes
and pixelates, fading to black,
with only the clock in the corner
still lit, flashing all zeroes, until
it vanishes as well.

Then, of course, all power
goes out, and I lose the lights,
and from the small office window,
I see even the sun go out.

Suddenly, I sense the loss of sound,
and all the whirring noises end—
sounds of machines, or of air
moving through the building's
many pipes—all have ceased.

Unnerving at first, this silence
grows more soothing,
and gradually, the darkness folds
me into itself and, coldly
but calmly, takes me
and holds me, on its own terms.

Odonata

Awaiting the estate agent,
he paces the empty house,
furnished, still, for the showing,
epiphany for someone else's plans.

He moves from room to room,
circling like a bird lost
above unfamiliar ground
far from the nesting site.

Like a bird, then, he alights
on the corner chair, from where
he sees the silence, today,
but hears past shadows moving.

The rooms seem larger than before,
but smaller, too, shape-shifting,
as if governed by uncertainty,
the arcane physics of memory.

Restless, he rises again, seeking
shelves with a few remaining books,
and at last his hand comes away
with a slightly brittle paperback—

The Concise Dictionary of Science—
his fingers brush across the cover,
its once-smooth surface covered now
with the sad patina of dust.

Paging through, aimlessly,
he happens upon the O's,
then pauses at an unfamiliar word
that sounds a magic spell— "Odonata"

Odonata, it says, the order of insects
for both dragon and damsel flies,
and suddenly his mind is freed
to breathless visions of danger and beauty

from old manuscripts or aging tapestries,
damsels protected only by their grace,
and dragons, being dragons, hungry
but still shy and reluctant to offend.

No knights to ride this insect world,
so damsels must defend themselves,
reaching accommodation with dragons,
who, after all, can be reasoned with.

Besides, no one really dies
on manuscripts and tapestries, no,
they merely chip away like old paint,
or unravel with the fragile threads.

There Is Nothing to Say

There is nothing to say—
this moment, now, with you,
is so fragile, so transient that
it can only be known but
never expressed or spoken . . .

even so, this knowledge, so
pointed, so poignant, must be
rejected, pushed away, if
we are to continue living, so
we look away, walk away

to leave knowledge for some
later day, some latter fate.
We know, nonetheless, that
one of us will, at that time
unspecified, be called to tasks

unwelcome and burdensome—
one of us will, inevitably, cast
down our gaze at the prostrate
other, in a gray room of tubes
and wires, with scrub-clad nurses

and a physician nodding gravely.
One of us will be called to meet
with officious staff for signatures,
and later with the graciously unctuous
men in funereal suits and quiet smiles

who can wrap and paint us pretty,
and place us boxed, and boxed again,
like a Russian nested doll into
the blank space of dull ground.
Or one of us will watch the other

be shelved like an old, unwanted
volume in the stacks for the rarely
used, or buried like a dead file
in the chambered, basement archives
deep under some nameless structure.

After days of rushing, half awake,
one of us will know the touch
of the front door knob, entering
familiar space without an answering
voice, merely the scent of the past.

There is nothing to say.

Transmigration of Souls

The ultimate commute,
truly, it's interminable—
old souls carted across eons,
traveling nightly through some
metaphysical underground.

You see, it's not as you'd imagined,
no glorious rolling clouds
suffused with golden light—
no, the real metaphysics
would surprise you with being
so ordinary and mundane.

For the souls, it seems
they travel in old transit cars,
faded blue outside, the inside
a pale yellow turning ashen,
and the chrome appointments
finger marked and oily.

The fates, it seems, are cheap,
and obsolete second-hand cars
make sense for tattered souls
of even older vintage—no matter,
the riders long ago stopped caring,
resigned to their awkward seats
on the slow ride to another life.

A motorman and transit cop
both keep silent watch,
while showing faces so blank
not even God can read them anymore,
expressions wiped away with time,
like old stones worn smooth.

The riders rest as they may, some
leaning back, dozing in their seats,
and others standing, holding the bar,
asleep, almost, on their feet—and each
dreaming of a sleep so deep
that its very dreams are sleep itself.

The older man in the corner,
coming off his stint as CEO,
with the residue of power
still staining his fingertips—God knows
what will become of him now,
but he shudders in his sleep.

That girl, chin drooping and
hat askew, barely eleven,
was murdered in some horrific crime,
but is thought to be coming back
a flower for a time, a restful life.

Old lady, standing, whose feet
still ache from endless work,
even now, she can barely reach
to hold the overhead bar—for her,
some ease at last, perhaps
some green and restful karmic park.

You get the idea—it goes on,
the long procession of days and nights,
moving as the darkened tunnel
seems to move backward
beyond the rattling windows.

It's late, and each is more tired
than any words could state—the car
shifts side to side, jarring some awake,
and they stare at the old faded posters,
the ads for some spiritual tonic,
or some fragrant soap to cleanse
a soul, and of course, the vacation
for two weeks in Nirvana, with
transportation and lodging included,
all for one unbelievably low price.

III. The Case History Monologues*

"A complete medical history includes a more in-depth inquiry into the patient's medical issues . . .." [Jonathan R. Nichol; Joshua Henrina Sundjaja; Grant Nelson. "Medical History." National Library of Medicine Website, NIH.]

In a "case history," the physician speaks of and for the patient. In these monologues, patients speak of and for themselves.

1. Clinical in Creve Coeur

October rain, endless,
provides establishing shots,
the opening sequence—I've seen
this film before and so have you,
but with no apology for the cliché,
the camera gives you
what we know of leaf-strewn streets viewed
through the car's rain-streaked windows—
classical music is dying on
the old radio, but though I want Barber
it is something else, a piece
I've never heard

Now the signs tell us
that we are in Creve Coeur,
where ranch houses sprawl
and doctors thrive
in anonymous low-rise offices,
hiding behind
the unrevealing glass—
I do not care if you like this film,
besides, I sold the story rights
long ago and far too cheaply,
having told the tale, week
by endless week,
through every season

My father once said
that a doctor's office used to
intimidate, with old
varnished paintings, and strong
chemical smells—not these,
he'd find them silly, the rose-colored
walls and pastel moods of furniture,
like ads for a week in a tropical place—
everyone wants to be calm, here, so

I am not excited and do not destroy
the mood, even when talking of how
my veins speak to me of somber colors
and how I sit, like a spider, in the
upper corner of the walls, spending
hours patiently watching myself

watch myself stare at my wrists,
as if the pulse were the visual effect
for a musical piece—like I said,
I'd want the Barber

The hour passed as hours pass,
like a story session, and she says,
I need to "re-script" my life, and
"stop rewriting the same cycle of
negative outcomes"—I feel like
a misbehaving corporation, with
unbalanced books and bad stock—
if I were a corporation, I would be
bankrupt for bad hair and ugly shoes

In the car, again, the wipers wipe,
the music calms the air, and
I see the signs—what ironic Frenchman,
centuries ago, named this place
"Broken Heart"? Did he bury
someone here, wife or child,
in soggy river ground?
Did he just not come up a winner
when trading with the tribes
(whose hearts no one cared for, ever)?
Creve Coeur, with its delicate
broken-heart logo—jaggedy crack
down the middle of the bright red
valentine, like an earthquake
on a greeting card.

2. Work-in-Progress

I am a work-in-progress,
not ready, yet, for exhibition,
but already I have shown other work—
my tattoos, for example,
a dragon on the right shoulder,
a dagger at the ankle, and a diamond
just above the butt—

And, of course, there are
the piercings, three in the right
ear, and four in the left—
I favor the left, you know,
I'm left handed, after all—
and, oh yes, one in each nostril,
one, finally, in the tongue.

Each session, she asks me
why I "punish" myself,
why do I cut—but I tell
her that I'm a sculptor,
the body is just my medium—
I cut the horizontal, which is
for revelation, and I cut
the vertical, which is
for transcendence, the lines
tell it all, tell everything.

In art history, last year,
we studied Michelangelo,
I wrote of his unfinished captives,
roughed out but incomplete,
struggling under the weight
of someone else's stone—
they'd have grabbed the chisel
right from his hands and cut
themselves free, if they could—
maybe I cut for them.
In the lit class, we read
Stephen Crane's poem where
a man finds the road to truth
covered over with weeds
but chose a different path

when he found each weed
was a knife—I see that road,
follow the knife-edged path,
and find there is very little blood,
if you do it right.

Your truth, my truth—
both written in a cramped script
of a million curling capillaries,
in a tongue few understand—
let me translate, here, on my arm,
see me make the curved line straight,
watch me simplify the truth
to a bright, linear red.

3. Understanding Depression

Waiting in the clinic exam room
I stare at wall posters like
"Understanding Depression,"
with its image of a young woman
pictured from waist up, head
bent downward, eyes staring
at something beyond the edge.
Framed by light-brown hair, her
imagined head reveals the brain beneath
with pale pink folds surrounding
inner structures, each labeled carefully.

At the very center, the thalamus sits,
white and ovoid, like some brooding
hard-boiled egg with shell removed,
communicating slowly with amygdalae,
those small clusters of mystery,
from which, the chart declares,
so much "negative emotion" flows.

A cheerful therapist arrives to ask
what symptoms have emerged—
"So how much stress do you have,
and how do you handle it now?"
Do you measure stress like some
negative energy in quantum physics?
Or like the atomic weight of heavy elements?
I would like to say I do not measure stress,
and if handle it I must, I do so gingerly.

Questions cease, she leaves, and I take
one last look at the sad-eyed poster,
noticing how the artist has drawn
several strands of hair that seem to fall
across the edges of the brain,
as if she had sensed, near the moment
of completion, that no one's thoughts
should ever be fully naked and revealed.

4. The Matter of Perception

I don't always see the same things,
don't always see the same way,
but then again, who does, really?
On my way from the train stop
to the clinic, I walk the whole time,
since it "does me good," according to
the doctor and his residents.

I could take the bus, but no,
it vibrates too much, shakes me,
rattles the brain and what mind
remains in residence there.
So I walk, north, the better part
of a mile, and see the sights—

Without the meds, I see buildings recede,
like skin on an aging skull, making
the windows, doors, and all the openings,
more prominent, more dangerous;
there were days I almost tortured myself
by knowing what each window held—
a face, a pair of eyes staring before
and after every step of mine, curious
to know what sins I carried
in the satchel of my soul.

With them, the meds that is,
it's different, perhaps better, calm
at least, serene? Or maybe, just vacant?
Yes, vacant, as if everyone had left,
moved out, driven away, leaving
the obvious open spaces of the lot,
and the hidden open spaces of lofts,
of offices, of apartments where
the parallel lines of bare wood floors
seem to stretch to infinity, especially
when you lie on them, looking at
the light too bright in the unshaded
window, light burning through
the glass, then through the eye as well.

Last month, there were problems,
"instabilities in the regimen,"
and my soul began to wobble
like a toy top losing its whirl,
losing its spin, waiting to fall—
the view changed then, and even
with all the demons gone, all the
skeletal faces in the staring windows
swept away, their strangeness remained,
and the buildings swelled and swayed,
as if inflated, as if they were balloons,
cartoonlike, laughable but scary—
they curved around themselves,
like the curve of the eyeball,
the curve of seeing, with something
unseen left waiting, around the curve,
beyond the eye's horizon.

5. Graveyard Shift

It's not like there's something wrong,
not like you'd think—no inner demon
willing me to kill or be killed
or produce direct-to-streaming tragedy—

what I hear is softer, a whisper
of secrets and the sound of shadows
sliding slowly over hollow space—
someone else's ghosts, not mine.

Some people broadcast themselves,
and I, despite myself, receive
an endless chain of repetitious fears,
the plainsong of pathetic histories.

At home, at night, the soft sounds
of furnaced air surrounding me,
I'd still find no peace, deafened almost
by the family's atonal dreams.

Now I work the graveyard shift at the
convenience store, as ghosts come and go,
some in awkward bodies, some in minds,
and a few, just a few, carried on the wind.

6. Street

I have seen and know things
that you have not—listen,
and I will tell you the secret
that the street is a river,
a river that rises first
in high ground, in distant hills—
clean, aloof, cold—
but cascading downward,
with each falling step, becomes
more angry and chaotic
till roiling with pain,
it flows merciless and deadly
through the city.

I, myself, have seen a thousand,
at least, vanish into
the opaque surface—
just today, I saw a man stand,
or try to stand, for one moment,
then disappear, less than smoke,
less than stains
that scatter themselves,
darkness on darkness
against the stones,
a river of stones, scarred with lye,
marked with tar, and each one
with its own strange story.

7. Sanctuary

He was awkward and old,
smelling musty in his age
like the smell of my grandmother's
attic on a hot summer day.

June mornings, suffused with light,
I walked to the sacristy and
donned black cassock and white surplice
to serve six-thirty Mass.

I was new to the "service"
and so assigned the earliest time,
when mostly no other boy would show,
leaving me to struggle on alone.

I was too short to light
the High Mass candles, could
make only lesser lights,
and besides, my Latin was weak.

He neither noticed nor cared,
nor did the three black-clad women
in front pews—like three fates
fingering my future in their beads.

Afterwards, I helped him with robes,
alb and chasuble, hung carefully,
the stole, kissed and folded with respect,
all amid a stale smell of wine.

A pause, and he turns to me,
"Now you must kiss me, boy."
It seemed but one more gesture,
one more ritual I need learn.

What did I know, amid such
strangeness—he from the "old country"
like the fated women in the pews,
all foreign mystery to me?

What did I know of strange
projections good only to pee with
or for some odd frisson of annoyance
and delight, purpose undisclosed?

Raised by women pious and devout,
who always were obsessed with cleaning house
I read of baseball, race cars, rockets,
not of human bodies and their parts.

Still, it seemed but one more touch
of all the mysteries that lingered
with the candle smells and holy cards—
a ritual kiss on sour unshaven cheek.

But my mother blanched when I had told,
questioned me, then called the nuns.
Thinking I'd broken once again
some hidden hygiene rule,

I feared punishment, but no need—
instead, I found myself with two weeks
free, then transferred to the 8 o'clock,
luxuriating in an extra hour's sleep.

With him sent back to old Italian hills,
no more was said, so I forgot—
and it was years before that moment
could have meaning worth a thought.

Only decades later, it dawned
what precipice he'd led me to,
but still, it seemed so small, his
errant call for my simple, frail lips.

So I imagine him, bound hand and foot,
at Vesuvius, the edge of Dante's hell,
so pathetic, lonely, self-condemned,
I cannot even hate him now.

8. Quiet

I moved through halls and
into rooms without speaking—
I just wanted to be quiet, myself,
in this noisy space, at last
having work to finish.

Because I have always kept
thoughts to myself, left
my voice unchallenged, now
they will stare at each silent face,
looking for a sign in the eyes,

Because I have preferred
my own company, now I have
made all solitude suspect and perverse—
the solitary reader in the corner
behind the library stacks,
the young man seated
at the far edge
of the athletic field, and
the girl who remains behind
in the empty classroom
—all will be scrutinized.

Since I carried this blue steel
and let it speak a few syllables
for me, naturally they will assume it
a substitute for frightened
sex or lost affection, hoping
by some theory to disarm me—
but it felt good in my hand,
hard and real, textured on the grip,
smooth and cold on the barrel.

They will judge me colder
than simple metal and
harsher than jacketed slugs
and ask how I could
move and act so calmly
amid screams and panic—
but I heard little but
the memory of flowing water

cascading through my mind,
fountain, stream, rapids and cataract,
that softened all to white noise.

I have nothing to say except
I wished to move slowly
and to cut through chaos,
or at least, to reveal it as it is,
set in swirling motion,
spiraling ever faster
away from me,
as I stood still and silent,
the empty space and vacuum
at its heart.

9. Excited

"This can work," I say,
"I can, I mean we can make this..."
but she just shakes her head slightly,
and sighs, you know that kind of
sigh that just means we're going nowhere,

and I know that it's because I get
excited and cannot stop talking,
often about the same thing, over and
over again and again, like a song
put on endless repeat and repeat,

and so I just keep at it, but still,
I know that I can get better at
listening and having conversations
that are normal, well almost, and
so I say, "I can make this work..."

but by then her mouth is a straight line,
neutral and unfeeling, like the anti-
happy face with the straight-line mouth,
and her eyes darken and 'fade to black'
as I call it, like the end of a noir film,

and so I say, out of the blue, that
"I wished you liked noir films the way
I do and then we could watch together,
you know, 'cause I know so much
about the old black-and-whites...'

but then I know that was the wrong
thing to say and she seems to retreat
away from me, and that's when I see
that bit of leaf on her sweater, on
her shoulder, and I try to not to look,

but I can't help it, you know, it
shouldn't be there, out of place and all,
so finally I reach over and sweep it
off with the back of my hand, and she
gives me that look and starts to move,

and she rises from her chair and turns,
walking straight for the café door,
so I'm surprised, and I'm always
surprised at how she moves so gracefully,
as if she could never make a false step,

then I want to follow, and getting up,
say all too loud in this public place
that "we can make this work . . ." but
I forget about the napkin tucked in my shirt,
and the coffee mug sitting on the table

left on the napkin's edge, and so when
I get up too quickly, the mug doesn't
just fall but does, like, a triple somersault,
sending spirals of coffee into the air,
on the café windows and floor, and even

all over my clothes, the cardigan's old,
but the shirt's the new one, so I'm so
shocked I trip and hit the table with
my knee, and it goes over with the bang
and crunch of wood on wood and shattered

glass and plates on wood, and all
the wood was what I liked about this place,
but now the waitress comes and glares
that special glare they save behind
their eyes for the world's worst

customers, like me, I guess, and then
the manager is there telling her to go,
and he's a nice Indian man, or maybe
Pakistani, or maybe both, if you can
be both, but now he's got the straight-

lipped non-smile and I'm saying "I'm
so sorry—I'll clean it up, I'll pay for . . ."
but he's calling me sir and asking me
to leave, and I just stare, not knowing
what to say for a minute, but then

I say, "Yes, yes, of course, I'll leave,
that's the best, but I'll be coming back
to pay and make it right . . ." but he's just
shaking his head, and I start to leave,
but add " it's 'cause I get excited. . . ."

10. Riddle of the Open Heart

I am a creature from an alien dream,
an image from some other galaxy,
where I dwelt in peace, deep
in my underground lake, afloat
in its currents, tranquil and slow.

A flood in reverse released me,
and cold hands received me,
leaving me in this nest of tubes,
with their blessings and curse—
I cringe in their mechanical embrace.

I cannot move in this airy cold,
and my vision is too frail
for anything but crude abstracts,
the blurred watercolor wash
of frantic animation.

I hear little but the sound
of breathing through my tube,
as if the wind took hold of me,
and made me shudder at its touch.

All this resolves itself, now,
to anxious faces I cannot read,
but still I sense their fear and awe,
a shiver that registers on fragile skin.

Their words, a mystery, still come,
and I feel them on my fingertips—
foreign words like "Premi" and "NICU,"
cold words but carried on
breath warmed by terror and hope.

Why have they trapped me
in this strange glass box,
an exotic fish in their prize aquarium?
What have they caught
that inspires such rapture?
I see only the mouths that open
like small black circles, so it is

they who are the large doubtful fish,
open-mouthed and wide-eyed,
floating in their ocean of questions.

Now they speak of the hole in my heart,
a frightening gap deep inside—
do they know, perhaps, the hidden dreams
that might seep out from me
to drown them in my sleep?

IV. In the Shadow of Corona*

---

*"It will take us many years to understand the long-term effects of COVID on our health, well-being, and way of life."
[Beth Jarosz, "The Long Shadow of COVID-19 on the U.S. Population." PRB (Population Research Bureau Website), May 3, 2022.]

Going Viral

It begins quietly, a faint buzzing,
a gnat or tiny fly at my ear,
or slightest whispering
of an angry rumor—clearly
this is not my problem.

Later, a loud image crawls past
my field of vision, fearful thing,
segmented, multi-legged and eyed,
but moving away—surely it will carry
its menace to corners far from me.

Then, one night, I wake to hear
a sound amplified, waves
rolling in, grinding stone against
stone on the angry shingle—
but peace, that tide is distant still.

Closing eyes, closing senses,
the mind still pictures, still hears
all the terror—of tubes and dials,
screens graphing pulse and pressure,
the slow machine's uncaring breath.

The Silence

[Spring, 2020]

Sudden, the silence was sudden, like
the hush in a room confronted with
a ghastly revelation—unexpected,

pervasive, all-encompassing, occupying
a space daily wider and more daunting,
daily spreading out, oceanic, even cosmic.

What planes? What cars or traffic?
The sky a clear blue without contrails,
highways uncluttered, lots empty.

What speech? What conversation?
Our words stopped flowing, the spring
of language frozen shut or clogged with debris.

Hidden in houses and rooms, staring
at uncaring screens bright with dark
messages, bright with vivid death.

Waiting, now, for the endpoint—will
it be over soon, over soon, please?
Waiting for night, or dawn, or deliverance.

A Social Distance

Mostly, now, we use social media,
screens filled with faces in boxes
like the old Hollywood Squares,
or a strange form of social prison.

Some carry on in closed offices—
you can hear their murmuring,
from time to time, like the sound
of mice running behind the wainscoting.

Halls, however, remain discretely
silent, except for the occasional
footstep or the distant sound of a door
closing, with the person still unseen.

The break room is empty, yet
the trace remains of someone who
left the microwave uncleaned and
also stole the disinfectant soap.

Sometimes, the lights and vents
are the only voices heard, their
soft-subtle rhythms like hymns
in dead languages of aging monks.

Six

The recommended distance
from one's breathe to another's,
with a mask of simple cloth
and the space of open air our shield.

The distance in miles from home
to that remembered place,
sectioned and sheltered by trees, but
cluttered and clotted with stones.

The enforced distance at the site,
guided by small, blue markers
spiked into hard but giving soil
beneath the tamped-down grass.

The number still allowed to watch
a slow and somber lowering,
six times six around the hole,
trying to square the circle of grief.

And last, a clichéd measurement
of downward motion into earthen dark—
of course, around us now
we always keep the space of graves.

Fragments in COVID Time

A First Covidelle* — 2020

The Hidden Thing

Unseen, unsensed, not even a slight
scent, too subtle for our belief,
still sharp enough to strike, to kill.

How Is This Happening?

It begins when we are looking
elsewhere, or sleeping, or making love—
silent, it rides breath deep into lungs.

Deaths and Rumors of Deaths

It's always far away, someone else's
tragedy, to us just evening news—
then our breath fades, the ambulance arrives.

Pandemic Declaration—03-11-2020

Enough bodies, side by side, in
white boxes, in dark earth, make
their own declaration—silenced voices speaking loud.

War Reporting

News video of E.R. and I.C.U.—
white sheets, blue gowns, pale walls—
monitors, ventilators are sounds of this battle.

Quiet

Silence, open sound space, no echoes—
few aircraft, occasionally the life-flight chopper—
even highway traffic noise, eternal, grows faint.

In Stasis

A clear day, no contrails cross
blue sky, no distant engine rumble—
absent wings, we must stay in place.

A Ration of Flour

Newly emptied shelves, a shot from
a dystopic film—I take the
last bag of flour, glad but guilty.

A Full Measure

Now, I measure space as never
before, six feet in all directions—
walking always within this sphere of distance.

Closure

I'd hoped for breakfast at Simon's
Deli but find only darkened windows—
in dim light, I see empty space.

Face

You speak my name, eyes alight,
voice inviting, but who are you
behind this mask of solid blue cloth?

Sign: "Handwashing—Best Practices"

More soap, hotter water, more deliberately
washing hands, like surgeons on television,
but counting down slowly, like launching missiles.

Sanitizer

None to buy, so I scrounge—
grain alcohol (190 proof), aloe, water—
cocktail for hands, stinging, "à votre santé."

Spaces

No challenge to park—large lot,
handful of cars—each vacant space
speaks absence, fear, as if awaiting apocalypse.

Catching Breath

Grey-haired woman, tubed and ventilated, expiring;
Black man, beneath white knee, choking;
we, watching the screen, mouths agape, gasping.

Drone's View

In beehives, playboy drones merely mate—
above cities, rotor drones fly on,
cameras showing vacant streets, revealing our absence.

Numbers

We follow the numbers, like stats
in a sport that counts only loss—
winning means being left to count again.

Curve of Space-Time

In the space of a year,
our cities opened streets to emptiness—
with faces covered, our eyes told all.

The "After"

The "before," the "normal," was delusion;
now, present terror flashes in darkness;
the "after" awaits, obscure, challenging our hope.

---

* [A "covidelle" is a new poetic form. It is a set of 19 Covid fragments, each of 19 words. A Covid Fragment should be 19 words in three lines, 6/6/7. A proper covidelle may deal with the experiences of the actual Covid-19 pandemic of 2019-2022+, or it may deal with other experiences of illness, suffering, loss, grieving, social unrest, political conflict, and systemic injustice that have been so prevalent in Covid times but in many other times as well.]

What Darkness May Come

[Autumn 2020]

Byron claimed darkness for his world,
hopeless beyond even the final man,
beneath the long, volcanic shadows
and piled dead of Napoleonic wars.

Yeats revealed his nightmare vision
of a rough beast driven to wake us
to the coming age, apocalyptic
without a light beyond the bloodied night.

Now we wake to early darkness,
as the season will demand, and
mourn the loss of evening sunlight,
anxious and fitful, afraid to sleep.

Each day, more shake with fever,
each night, more rasp the clotted breath,
alone in grey-lit rooms, comforted only
by gowned ghosts, by tubes and wires.

Speak "hope" and the word falls and fails,
the grim air too heavy and thick to carry it,
so say nothing, listen to the slow decline,
but keep silence the final sacred space.

Birdman

[The 17th-century plague doctor in the bird-like mask.]

Beaked malevolence, inhuman mask,
black-clad like the hungry reaper,
but less passionate—objective, clinical—
his purpose to confirm the fates, approving
how those crone sisters measure out and cut.

Herbs, they say, cowered at the beak's
end, to counter evil vapors, miasma
of God's wrath or demon's desire—
the man, all leather, deep-dyed, gloved,
hatted, and caped for the endgame.

What sights came through goggled eyes,
what wet breath gathered within and
fogged the brain, while the heart rushed,
having seen the bodies deconstruct to pus
and blood and gasping foul air?

Having heard the moans and cries,
the weeping terror down city alleys,
having smelled the most human scent
of morbid, mortal flesh to its last—
nowhere left for the birdman to fly.

Descent into the Underworld

In Memory of Those We've Lost—2020-22

Ancient singers, indigenous tellers,
they know the need to leave sense behind
and descend, level by level, a dark path.

The hero's call is downward first,
as Odysseus and Aeneas, though enemies,
both knew and sought to answer.

Even the Christ we learn in scriptures
bows to necessary descent to find
long-awaiting righteous souls

and call them from curled spirit
slumbers to wake and rise and speak,
then sing in chorus on a higher plane.

We try to rise but stumble,
yet darkness then is more cure
than curse, to see soul's ambient light.

We cannot follow, Dante-like,
the faltering steps to that strangeness,
so we follow in memory and hope

those whose past light seemed bright,
and whose bodies' descent and loss
cut deep pain in our many minds.

We follow, now, descending into grief,
the daylight shrouded, the nights unlit,
as if no one or nothing sparked a flame.

We mourn, we cry, we shout
the threnodies, sing the melodies of loss
and pain that echo from ancients to our ears,

and yet, we find, in those echoes,
new presence beyond fear or even hope,
find the upward curve past hard descent.

What Will You Remember?

What, what will you remember when
we, awkward and uncertain, try
to keep your memory sharp and clear?

Will it be the forked branch that
roughly brushed your smooth skin, once,
on the red-brick path of the garden?

Will it be the weight and heft
of that heavy bag, over the left
shoulder, after a long day, or

will it be the sweaty palms
and fingers of your left hand
as you, fatigued, grasped the strap?

Perhaps it will be the firm touch
of the key in your right hand
as you opened the red front door,

or the sigh that escaped you when
you saw the boys' room in disarray
and a sink filled with dishes,

or how the sun looked, slanting through the
kitchen window, patterning the counter
as you prepared the supper.

Maybe it would be the other sigh
you gave, when all others were abed,
and you in darkness sipped that lone drink,

or even the silent relief you felt,
head touching pillow, as you found sleep
not merely a release but an earned reward.

You fade from us, evaporate, like the
low mist on a warm September morning,
and at times we wonder if you were real.

What is your memory, if you are
but memory to those you left, and will we
cease to be if you do not remember us?

When It Will Come

When it will come, it will come
as it may, as it can, through a will
of its own, its time and form still
uncertain and obscure—but how?

Will it be sudden and harsh,
like the ambulance in the night,
racing onward, red and white,
with sirens and lights slicing the dark?

Or like the pick-up, drunk-driven
wrong way on the Interstate,
speeding past ninety, directly
through me and toward oblivion?

Maybe it comes silent but sharp,
like the spider hidden between
baseboard and wall, waiting
with menace, multi-legged, multi-eyed.

Or will it be from the stored-up rage
of the "good man" next door,
who stokes his anger and strokes
his gun, till bullets speak his piece?

Perhaps, though, the fault will be
my own—the clumsy foot upon the stair
or in the shower, or distracted motion
crossing a familiar but high-trafficked road.

Or will it be the secret space within,
where the stubborn clot swims fast
upstream to clog the aging heart
or blow apart a vessel in the brain?

Will it be the virus and its vast horde,
mechanistic and deliberate, swarming
the system, overcoming all defense,
destroying cell by helpless cell?

Or will betrayal come from cells
themselves that collude and conspire
in darkness, to craft a certain death
from out the very source and form of life?

It will come as it may, as it can, any
moment, any motion the time or cause—
so we carry it within and carry on without,
knowing, always, what we are but wish not to be.

Where Is the Shadow?

Where is the shadow
that once you left behind
in the late sunlight
of a winter afternoon?
I know I saw it drawn clearly then
across the bare hardwood floor.

Has it slipped beneath the bed,
rolled with those old posters,
their ragged edges gathering dust,
or in those long flat boxes
where you kept the trophies
from your victories at school?

Was it left in the closet,
where the old uniform hangs,
crisp under taut plastic,
along with three generations of ties,
wide or narrow, subdued or loud,
or even in the shoes tightly closed
in a neat row of cardboard boxes?

Perhaps it passed down the stairs,
into the hall or living room,
or waits at the dining room table,
near that growing pile of mail,
or even in the kitchen, against the counter,
expecting empty cups to be filled?

I fear that, cleaning one day
and shaking rugs from out the window
on the second floor, mistakenly
I cast it out into the loamy garden,
among the stalks of last year's flowers,
beneath the layers of fallen leaf and seed.

Lethe

No sting, no ache
in rain so warm,
so soft that, walking
in it, even for hours,
I feel no chill,
only a new nakedness
without fear.

Once I had been
rushing to leave somewhere
and reach somewhere else,
but now I forget,
and sensing light
behind layers of cloud,
I make this rain
my new home.

Additional Acknowledgments

The following poems have been published in periodicals as listed below. The author gratefully acknowledges the support of these earlier publications.

"As If Secrets Would Spill" (*Chautauqua*, 2022)
"The Ceremony of Innocence" (*La Piccioletta Barca*, 2023)
"What the Bullet Knows" (*St. Louis Anthology*, Belt Press, 2019)
"In the Heat of the Moon" (*The Write Launch*, 2021)
"Emergency Procedure Guide "(*St. Louis Poetry Center 54th Annual Poetry Concert*—Chapbook, 2013)
"Never Send . . ." (*The Bellevue Literary Review*, 2019)
"Carbon Content" (*Work*, 2016)
"Life of the Ball Turret Gunner" (*Please See Me*, 2020)
"This Poem Is Just about You" (*The Healing Muse*, 2021)
"Respiratory Monitor" (*Lifelines*, 2018)
"Call It" (*Medicine and Meaning*, 2023)
"When He Died in His Sleep" and "Everyman Revisited" (*St. Louis Poetry Center 55th Annual Poetry Concert*—Chapbook, 2014)
"There Is Nothing to Say" (*Medicine and Meaning*, 2023)
"Transmigration of Souls" (*Snapdragon: A Journal of Art & Healing*, 2022)
"Clinical in Creve Coeur" and "Work-in-Progress" (*The Examined Life*, 2011)
"The Matter of Perception" (*Blood and Thunder*, 2017)
"Street" (*Mingled Voices 5*—Proverse Press Anthology, 2020)
"Excited" (Published as a flash fiction in *Lifelines*, 2022)
"Riddle of the Open Heart" (*Blood and Thunder*, 2017)
"A Social Distance" (*Mingled Voices 6*—Proverse Press Anthology, 2022)
"Six" (*Blood and Thunder*, 2021)
"Fragments in COVID Time" (*Blood and Thunder*, 2023)
"What Darkness May Come" (*Blood and Thunder*, 2021)
"Where Is the Shadow?" (*Blood and Thunder*, 2021)
"Lethe" (*Natural Bridge*, 2014)
"Going Viral" (*Ariel's Dream*, 2021)
"In the Sunlight" and "Graveyard Shift"—as "Night at the Convenience Store" (*One Art*, October 31, 2024)
"The Mummy's Curse" (*The Petigru Review*, Fall 2024)
"Specific Gravity" (*Corporeal*, Volume XVIII, 2024)
"Mystic Chords of Memory" (*Corporeal*, Volume XVIII, 2024)
"The Silence" (*The Closed Eye Open*, Issue VII, June, 2022, 65)
"Chicago View" (*The Closed Eye Open*, Issue XIII, 2025)
"Sanctuary" (The Healing Muse, Vol. 25, 2025)

Vincent Casaregola teaches American literature and film, creative writing, and rhetorical studies at Saint Louis University. He has published poetry in a number of journals, including *2River, The Bellevue Literary Review, Blood and Thunder, The Closed Eye Open, Dappled Things, The Examined Life, The Healing Muse, Lifelines, Natural Bridge, Please See Me, WLA, Work,* and T*he Write Launch*. He has also published creative nonfiction in *New Letters* and *The North American Review*.

Casaregola has been writing and publishing poetry and other genres, on and off, for several decades, but the past decade or so has been his longest sustained period of production. Having to deal with issues of chronic, serious illness among a number of family members and friends, he began writing frequently about the issues of health and illness, along with the experience of loss and grieving. The poetry in *Vital Signs* has grown from these experiences, and, more recently, from the COVID pandemic. Hospitals and doctors' offices, patient rooms and waiting rooms are the sites from which these poems emerge, as well as from the homes where empty space has replaced the presence of family members. He also works in literary nonfiction and fiction. In collaboration with colleagues at the Saint Louis University School of Medicine, he is working to develop a new journal devoted to creative writing about illness and medicine.

Additionally, Casaregola engages in scholarly writing about film, media studies, and American cultural history, areas that he also teaches in at Saint Louis University. Along with a number of scholarly articles and book chapters in these areas, he has published a book-length work on the American literature and film of World War II (*Theaters of War: America's Perceptions of World War II*, Palgrave-Macmillan, 2009). He is currently at work on a new scholarly book project about American film of the 1950s. From 1994 through 2007, he served as the First-Year Writing Program Director in the English Department at Saint Louis University, and from 2013-2019, he also served as Director of the Film Studies minor in the College of Arts and Sciences there.

Casaregola lives in St. Louis, MO, with his spouse, Victoria Carlson-Casaregola, who is a writer and a speech-language pathologist. They have two grown daughters, Maya and Marina.

www.ingramcontent.com/pod-product-compliance
Lightning Source LLC
Chambersburg PA
CBHW030053170426
43197CB00010B/1514